A TREASURE CHEST OF JOKES AND RIDDLES

by
Chris Tait

Copyright © 2004 Kidsbooks, LLC
230 Fifth Avenue
New York, NY 10001

Manufactured in the United States of America

0104-1CW

Visit us at www.kidsbooks.com

Contents

Aaargh, Here Be Pirate Jokes!

Why did the pirate go on vacation?

Because he needed some AARRRRGGH and AARRRRGGH! (R and R)

What do you call a pirate with a wooden leg?

I don't know, I'm stumped!

What do you say to a pirate who is lost in the woods during winter?

"Shiver me timbers!"

How much does it cost a pirate to get a piercing?

A buck an ear! (buccaneer)

What do you call a one-legged pirate who is a traitor?

Mutin-knee! (mutiny)

What do you call a pirate
who skips school?

Captain Hooky!

Where do pirates like to
leave their ships?

In Aaaaargh-gentina! (Argentina)

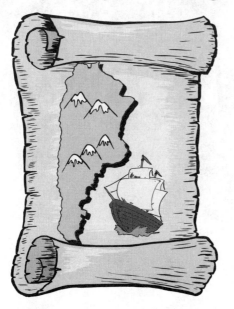

How did the one-eyed pirate feel
when he squinted?

A little patchy!

Why did the pirate learn to
play the violin?

So he could fiddle around!

What do a pirate and Santa Claus have in common?

They both say, "Ho, ho, ho!"

⚓

What kind of animal do pirates like best?

Aaaargh-varks!

What does a pirate who farms have on his land?

A barn-icle! (barnacle)

What kind of cookies do pirates eat?

Ships Ahoy!

What do pirates do at Halloween?

They go out trick or looting!

A pirate walks into his favorite restaurant. "I haven't seen you in a while," the waiter says. "What happened to you?"

"What do you mean?" asks the pirate. "I'm fine."

"What about that wooden leg?" the waiter says. "You didn't have that before."

"I was in a battle at sea and a cannonball hit my leg. But the doctor fixed me up with this wooden leg, and I'm fine."

"OK," says the waiter. "But what about that hook? The last time I saw you, you had both of your hands."

"Well," says the pirate, "I was in a sword fight and my hand was cut off. But the doctor fixed me up with this hook, and I feel great."

"OK," the waiter says. "But what about that eye patch? The last time I saw you, you had both of your eyes."

"Well," the pirate says, "one day when we were at sea, some birds were flying over the ship. I looked up, and one of them pooped in my eye."

"You couldn't have lost an eye from some bird poop!" The waiter exclaims.

"No," says the pirate, "but I wasn't used to the hook yet!"

What do you say when you beat a pirate at chess?

"Check, matey!"

What do you call a pirate who has a small piece of wood stuck in his finger?

Long John Sliver!

What do you call a pirate's wife?

Peggy!

How did the pirate get his ship
so cheap?

He bought it on sail!

What's the best part about a pirate joke?

The hook!

Pirate Pals

What do you call a parrot that looks just like its pirate owner?

A chick off the old block!

What do you say to a parrot who thinks he's a duck?

"Polly want a quacker?"

What kind of cats do pirates like?

Saber-toothed tigers!

What do you call a pirate who loves to swim in the sea?

Sharkbait!

What do you call a parrot who is a bully?

A mocking bird!

What has eight hands and eight legs?

Eight pirates!

What did the pirate say about the dirty bird?

"Somebody swab that duck!"

Where do piranhas learn to be vicious?

In schools, of course!

**A pirate tried to attack his parrot.
What was he arrested for?**

Fowl play!

**Did the pirate have fun when he fell into the water
with the humpbacks?**

*Yes, he had a whale
of a time!*

What do a pirate and his parrot play when they are bored?

Hide and screech!

**What did the parrot do when
it heard that a monkey was coming aboard?**

He went ape!

Pirate Pete, who was very competitive,
saw that his best pirate friend had
a bigger, more colorful parrot than he did.
So Pete decided to get an even bigger,
more colorful bird, with an enormous
beak. Do you know what Pete said to his
friend when he returned with his new bird?

"Toucan play at that game!"

How did the pirate get along with the tuna?

Swimmingly!

What is more dangerous than a pirate with a sharp blade?

A swordfish, of course!

Which birds are the easiest to fool on ships?

The sea gull-ibles!

Which pirate birds are the best singers?

The parrots of Penzance! (The Pirates of Penzance)

Knock knock!
Who's there?
A parrot!
A parrot who?
A parrotly, you have no idea!

Knock knock!
Who's there?
Whale!
Whale who?
Whale you just let me in so I can show you?

What did the tuna say to the other fish?

"I may be lost at sea, but I will never flounder!"

Why are mollusks so quiet?

Because they always seem to clam up!

**What did the lobster say
about the mean shellfish?**

"Why is he so crabby?"

What did the pirate call the parrot's predictions about rain?

The feather forecast!

What do you get when you cross a parrot with a shark?

I don't know, but be careful or it'll talk your ear off!

What did the pirate call her parrot when it was arrested?

A jailbird!

Three silly sailors were stranded on an island. One day, they found a lamp in the sand. They rubbed it and out came a genie, offering to give them one wish each.

The first sailor asked to be strong. Instantly, he was filled with energy. He jumped in the water and swam to shore.

The second sailor asked to be fast. Immediately, he too jumped in the water and swam to the shore in no time flat.

The third sailor asked to be smart. He stood up, thanked the genie, and walked across the bridge to land.

Why can't you make
a parrot sing in key?

*For the same reason that you
can't tune a fish!* (tuna fish)

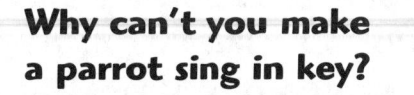

What bird can eat the most,
even though it's so small?

The swallow, of course!

What do pirates call a dangerous ten-armed creature?

Captain Squid!

How did the pirates know that they had been betrayed by their albatross?

Because it had switched tides on them!

27

How do you know if dolphins are saying hello?

By their waves!

What is a pirate's favorite sandwich?

Peanut butter and jellyfish!

What song did the pirate sing to lure the fish?

"Salmon-chanted Evening"!

Which shellfish is the most lonely?

The hermit crab!

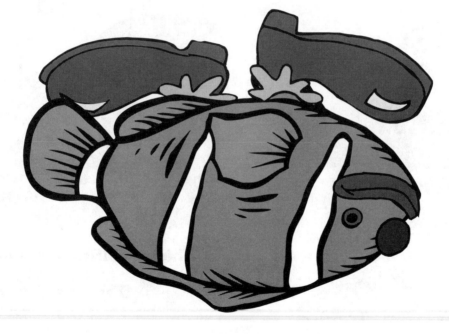

What type of fish always makes a pirate giggle?

A clownfish!

Treasure Pleasure

What do you call a pirate snoozing on top of a treasure chest?

Sleeping booty!

Why didn't the pirate like to see his treasure tied down?

Because it made his chest tight!

How did the pirate feel when he saw
his treasure at the bottom
of the ocean?

It gave him a sinking feeling!

How do you know you've found
a pirate's cooking bowl?

When X marks the pot!

**What did the pirate call his
smelly hoard?**

Skunken treasure!

How can you tell what's inside a treasure chest?

Easy, just shake your booty!

**What did the pirate
call her lost scales?**

Buried measures!

How do pirates cook with treasure?

On the trove top!

Knock, knock!
Who's there?
Barry!
Barry who?
Barry-ed treasure! (buried)

What did the one pirate, who didn't know where the treasure was, say to the other pirate who did?

"Go ahead, get it off your chest!"

**What is a pirate's favorite letter
of the alphabet?**
Arrrrrrrr!

**What did the pirate say to his friend
when he saw a map lying out on the deck?**

"Why don't you and I go take a scroll!"

What do you call a skeleton that guards treasure?

Finder's creepers!

What do you call a pirate who spends her treasure on new glasses?

Golden eye!

**What did the pirate say about
the X on the spot?**

"I can dig it!"

**How do you know when a map is
going to lead you to mutiny?**

When the X is double-crossed!

Two thirsty pirates were stranded on their ship with nothing to drink. Suddenly, a lamp bumped up against the side of their vessel. The first pirate pulled it out of the water and rubbed it. A genie popped out and offered to grant them one wish.

The first pirate said, "I wish the ocean were full of cold milk to drink!"

Suddenly, all around the boat, they were surrounded by a sea of delicious white milk.

"Way to go!" said the second pirate. "Now what are we going to use for a bathroom?"

What do you call shoes for baby pirates?

Booties!

What do you call a pirate's knapsack?

A loot bag!

What did the greedy pirate drink out of?

A gobble-it! (goblet)

What did the treasure-hungry pirate name his daughter?

Ruby!

41

What did the treasure-hungry pirate name his son?

Jules! (jewels)

What did the pirate's fortune do when the treasure chest sank?

It took a dive!

Why did the pirate go on strike when he couldn't open the lock on the treasure chest?

Because he felt that he had to pick it! (picket)

Why did the pirate get lost looking for treasure in Africa?

He thought that he was supposed to follow the dotted lion! (dotted line)

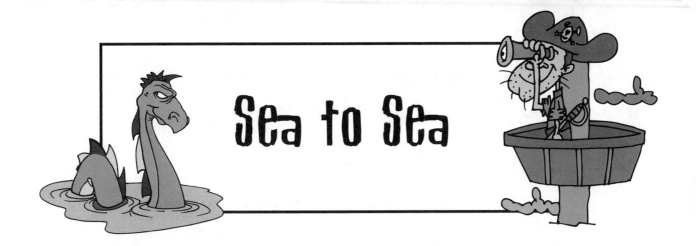

Sea to Sea

Where did the band of pirates find the ghost?

In the Dead Sea!

Why did the pirate keep doing the backstroke?

Because he didn't want to swim on a full stomach!

How do slow pirates swim for the shore?

By doing the crawl!

How do pirates do in school?

Their grades are always at sea level! (C level)

Why do pirates love salt water?

Because pepper makes them sneeze!

Why do seagulls live by the sea?

*Because if they lived by the bay,
they'd be called bagels!*

**How did the pirate complain
about the fish he had caught?**

He carped about it!

45

Knock, knock!
Who's there?
Shellfish!
Shellfish who?
Shellfishness will get you
nowhere. Let me in!

Knock, knock!
Who's there?
Kelp!
Kelp who?
Kelp me, I'm freezing out here!

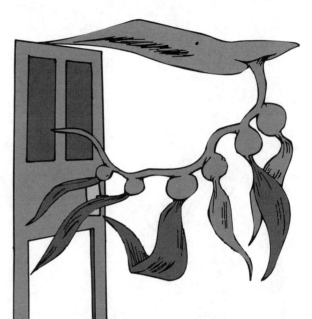

A bunch of pirates was building a pirate ship in the harbor. One of them noticed an old pirate in his swimming trunks, climbing up the ship. He had a floaty around his waist and was making his way toward the plank. One pirate called out to him, "Don't jump, there's no water here!"

"That's all right," the old pirate answered. "I can't swim!"

How did the fish eggs get to shore?

They just roe-d! (rowed)

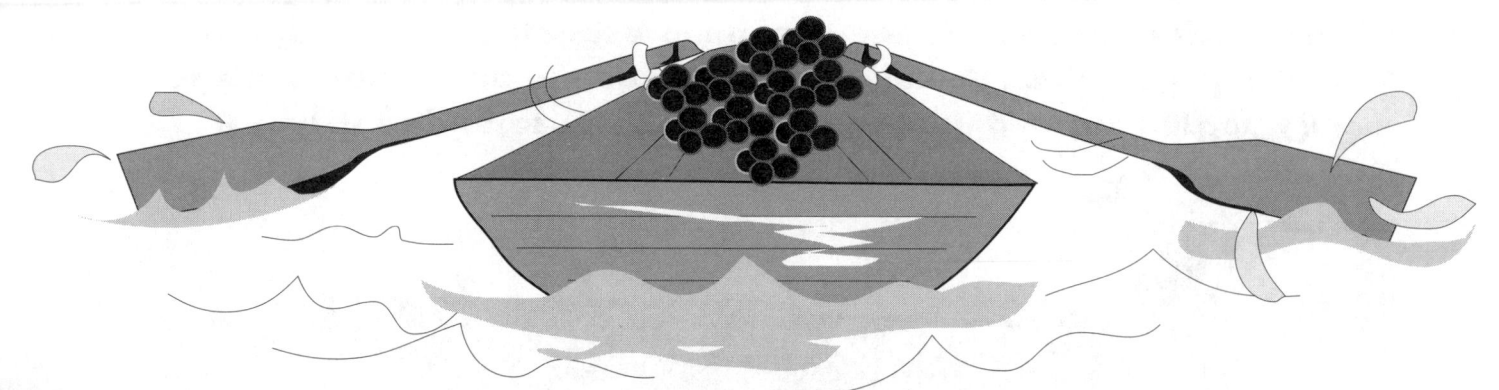

How did the pirate stop the fishheads from smelling up the deck?

He plugged their noses!

Where did the silly pirate think fish came from?

Finland!

What did the tough shellfish say to the other shellfish?

"My mussels are bigger than yours!"

What do you find at the bottom of scared oceans?

Nervous wrecks!

Why did the lobster rush to the rescue?

Because it hated to see a clamshell
in distress!

How do little fish get to school?

On the octo-bus!

50

What do deep-sea monsters love to eat?

Fish and ships!

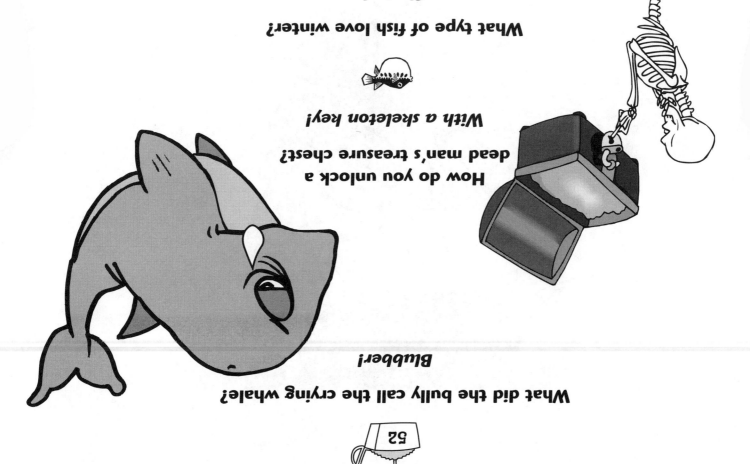

What type of fish love winter?

Skates!

How do you unlock a dead man's treasure chest?

With a skeleton key!

What did the bully call the crying whale?

Blubber!

Why did the sea creature wish that it looked sharper?

Because it was a dull fin!

Why are pirates such good fisherman?

Because they have the best hooks!

How can you identify a leopard fish?

Oh, they're easy to spot!

Where do fish dip their pens?

In squids, of course!

What's the worst part about living at the bottom of the sea?

The pressure!

Genie-us!

Why was the genie angry?

Because he felt bottled up!

What did the genie break when she fell out of her lamp?

Her wishbone!

Three pirates were stranded on a desert island for many years. One day, a golden lamp washed ashore. The first pirate rubbed it and a genie appeared, stretching out on a puff of blue smoke.

"I will give you one wish each," the genie said.

The first pirate spoke quickly. "I want to be back home eating a great meal in England!"

Just like that, he found himself in England, at his favorite restaurant, eating his favorite meal.

The second pirate said, "I wish I was back in America, eating a cheeseburger!" Just like that, he too was home.

Then the third pirate spoke up. "I'm going to be awfully lonely now. I wish the other two pirates were still here!"

Knock, knock!
Who's there?
Genie!
Genie who?
Genie-us! (genius)

Why do genies need housekeepers?

To take care of the magic dust!

What is a genie's favorite song?

"When You Wish Upon a Star"!

What do you call the most powerful genie of all?

Whatever she wants you to!

What do genies wear when they get out of the tub?

Their magic towels!

What did the surfer think when the genie turned her into a frog?

She thought it was toad-ally awesome!

What did the genie say when he granted a wish to a snake?

Abra-da-cobra!

What did the woman say when the genie told her how much it would cost to grant her wish?

"That's a charm and a leg"!

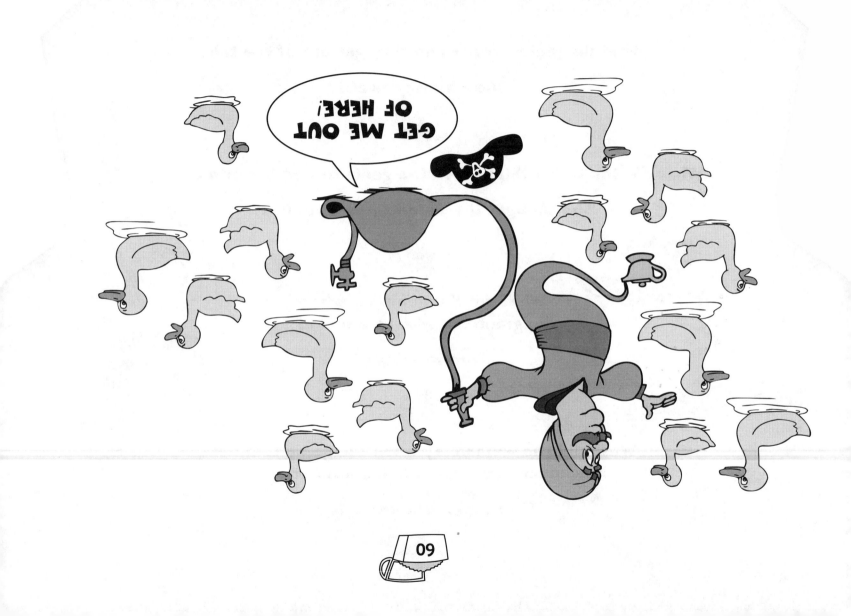

A pirate found a genie on the beach, sitting outside of his lamp.

"Do you grant wishes?" the pirate asked.

"I used to," said the genie, "but I retired."

"Why is that?" said the pirate.

"Well, I can't hear so well and it makes my job difficult."

"But can you still grant wishes?" asked the pirate.

"Sure," said the genie. "I'll give you two."

"All right," said the pirate. "I'd like a million bucks!"

Suddenly, there was a puff of smoke and the pirate found himself surrounded by a million quacking ducks.

"No, no," he said. "I said *bucks*, not *ducks*."

The old genie just shrugged.

"All right, for my second wish, I want to be in a giant house!"

There was another puff of smoke. When it faded away, the genie looked at the wriggling green bump beside him.

"It's going to take him forever to get out of that hose," the genie said.

A goofy man was stranded on an island, dying of thirst. Suddenly, a lamp washed on shore. He rubbed it and a genie appeared, offering him two wishes.

"I wish for a bottle of water that will never be empty!"

Sure enough, in his hand appeared a bottle full of cold, clear water. He quickly opened the top and drank until he could drink no more and, still, the bottle was full.

"Well," said the genie. "How was that?"

"Great," said the man. "I wish I had another one!"

Why do genies like alphabet soup?

Because they can spell while they eat!

What did the genie say about his wife's latest spell?

She was in a cast for weeks!

How do you get rid of a genie?

You just rub him out!

Knock-knocks for Knuckleheads

Knock, knock!
Who's there?
Izzy!
Izzy who?
Izzy coming out or should I come in?

Knock, knock!
Who's there?
Sara!
Sara who?
Sara 'nother time I should come back?

Knock, knock!
Who's there?
Don Juan!
Don Juan who?
Don Juan to go to school today, let's go to the zoo!

Knock, knock!
Who's there?
Ollie!
Ollie who?
Ollie told me was to knock!

Knock, knock!
Who's there?
Ken!
Ken who?
Ken I come in or are you gonna leave me out here all day?

Knock, knock!
Who's there?
Sam!
Sam who?
Sam day, you'll remember!

Knock, knock!
Who's there?
Cello!
Cello who?
Cello dere, dahling, how ah you?

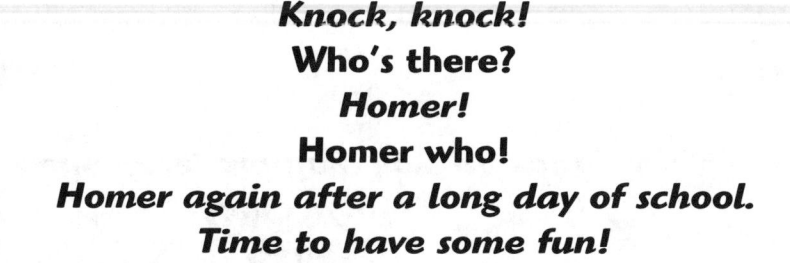

Knock, knock!
Who's there?
Homer!
Homer who!
Homer again after a long day of school.
Time to have some fun!

Knock, knock!
Who's there?
Everest!
Everest who?
Everest your eyes during the middle of class?
Teachers hate that!

Knock, knock!
Who's there?
Harold!
Harold who?
Harold are you, anyway?

Knock, knock!
Who's there?
Heidi!
Heidi who?
Heidi claire, something smells delicious!

Knock, knock!
Who's there?
Emma!
Emma who?
Emma too early for lunch?

Knock, knock!
Who's there?
Juanita!
Juanita who?
Juanita sandwich with me!

Knock, knock!
Who's there?
Jimmy!
Jimmy who?
Jimmy a chance and let me in!

Knock, knock!
Who's there?
Amy!
Amy who?
Amy 'fraid I may have the wrong house.
You don't sound familiar at all!

Knock, knock!
Who's there?
Doughnut!
Doughnut who?
Doughnut make me reveal my
true identity. I'm undercover!

007

TOP SECRET

Knock, knock!
Who's there?
Seek!
Seek who?
Seek-ret agent double-oh-seven!

Knock, knock!
Who's there?
Ray!
Ray who?
Ray member the last time
I was here?

Knock, knock!
Who's there?
Wendy
Wendy who?
Wendy clock strikes twelve, it's lunch time!

Knock, knock!
Who's there?
Tommy!
Tommy who?
Tommy you'll always be special! (to me)

Knock, knock!
Who's there?
Desk!
Desk who?
Desk-ribe yourself and maybe I'll tell you!

Knock, knock!
Who's there?
Alfred!
Alfred who?
Alfred duh needle if you'll tie the knot!

Knock, knock!
Who's there?
Roberts!
Roberts who?
Roberts are afraid of alarms!

Knock, knock!
Who's there?
Douglas!
Douglas who?
Douglas is broken. They must have come in at night!

Knock, knock!
Who's there?
Raymond!
Raymond who?
Raymond me again what I'm doing here!

Knock, knock!
Who's there?
Emma!
Emma who?
Emma bugging you yet?

Knock, knock!
Who's there?
Howell!
Howell who?
Howell I ever get in if you don't know who I am?

Knock, knock!
Who's there?
Disguise!
Disguise who?
Disguise are killing me with these knock-knock jokes!

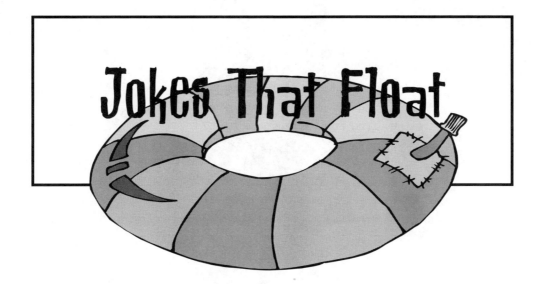

Jokes That Float

What did they call the pirate who stole a sailboat?

The mast avenger!

What is the best kind of party to have on a pirate ship?

A mast-erade party!

Why did the pirate stop his ship near the tropical island?

Because he had a h-anchoring for some coconuts!

What do pirates use to blow their noses?

Anchor-chiefs!

Why did the little sailor tie down his sails?

Because he was just feeling knotty!

What did the lazy sailor say when his boat became untied?

"Glad I'm knot in charge!"

Why did the sea captain decide to retire from his career?

Because sails weren't what they used to be!

How did the captain get the sailor to mop up?

He threatened to deck him!

What do you call it when a comet hits the deck of a ship?

Starboard!

What did the fish play after school?

Trout or dare!

What did the pirate say when the cat caught the mouse?

Micely done!

Why did the sailor throw his oar in the sandbar?

Because he wanted to try surf 'n' turf!

Why did the captain want to run his boat back and forth to shore?

Because he still believed in ferries!

Why was the sailor looking for his boat in the snow?

Because he heard it was a drift!

How can you save your supper from drowning?

Dip it in a gravy boat!

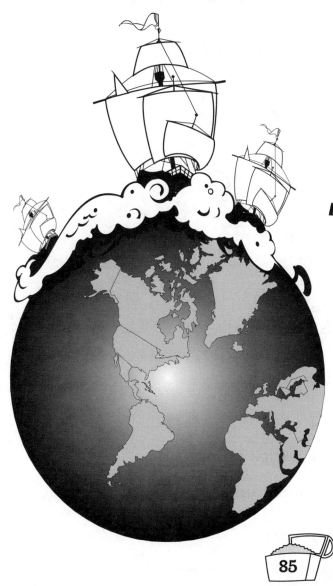

Why did the sailor want to navigate around the world?

Because he heard it was all in compassing! (encompassing)

What happened when the boat sank in a school of sharks?

It ended up with a skeleton crew!

98

How did the boat get cuddly?

It hugged the shoreline!

Why was the sailor mad at his leaky-bottomed boat?

Because he knew that he would have to get stern with it!

What did the pirate call his country house?

The skull and cross barns!

⚓

What did the sailor say to his dog?

"Good buoy!"

Why did the sailor fall into the harbor?

*Because he wasn't playing
with a full dock!*

What did the captain say about his
leaky boat?

"It was a bit of a drip!"

What song did the king sing as he paddled around his castle?

"Row, Row, Row Your Moat"!

What color clothes do people stranded on a desert island wear?

Maroon!

What do you call a ship's gunner if he has no hair?

Cannon-bald!

What do you call a ship's kitchen when it isn't clean?

The same as ever—a mess!

93

What grade do navigators need in order to graduate?

A com-pass!

How do sailors find their way around if they become cowboys?

They just follow the north steer!

What did the sailor think about these jokes that float?

He said they didn't hold water!

JOKES THAT FLOAT